Dung Beetles
and
Butterflies

*Poetry from all kinds of crap
to evolving growth and beauty*

KRISTINA KEITH

ISBN Paperback: 979-8-9888877-0-6
ISBN Ebook: 979-8-9888877-1-3

Design and publishing assistance
by The Happy Self-Publisher.

Table of Contents

To everyone that helps keep poetry alive,
Thank you.

Jerrica Clark, my daughter,
personal critic, my artist
Thank You
I Love you!

Write On!

Buffet of emotions

Marinated in madness
Seasoned with sadness
A dash of shame
A pinch of pain
Battered in vulnerability
Glazed in Humility
Steamed in stress
Broiled in boldness
Fried with joy
Baked in Beauty
Grilled with Glee
Sprinkled with love
Now serving me

Who I once was

Made mistakes, many
Change some, not any
Where I was, reminder of where not to go
Where I am going, still left to be known
Who I once was, not who I am
Being labeled from the past, a future scam
Who I am now, incomplete
Who I was yesterday, the only one with whom I compete

To Conquer

To conquer does not always mean another you have defeated
To some, true triumph would be cycles not repeated
Tackling responsibilities, marking them completed
standing tall, although mistreated
nurturing all that come to you without getting depleted
keeping hate away, knowing its deep seated
when alone, I wonder, would I be so strong
if my Trauma deleted

I Will for You

I could leave you the fast car I use to drive,
Instead, I leave you my caring for others that really
made me thrive.

I could leave you a check and leave it blank,
Instead of more value, I leave the ability to wait for
emotions to pass before your next move you think.

I could leave you all the clothes I wore to
make me look attractive,
Instead, I leave you my desire to find free beauty
in the world to hold you captive.

I could leave you all the nice Knick knacks I collected
throughout the years,
Instead, I leave permission to allow yourself the
release of held back tears.

I could leave you all the answers to tough
questions I honestly gathered,
Instead, I leave you with strength to seek your own,
determining what really mattered.

I could leave you with the last expensive thing
I bought at a store,
Instead, I leave you confidence to let your
creativeness soar.

I could leave you all my money I earned along the way,
Instead, I leave you my hope to spend on another day.

Beer joint buddies

Whoever brought the biggest bottle usually
has the most sitting at their table.
The ones telling you everything they are going to do, keep
drinking, making them unable.

Loudest one in the crowd needs the most attention,
obviously getting it nowhere else.
The ones saying, I love you! after every shot,
doesn't even love their self.

The ones saying, I will kick your ass!
can barely carry their own.
The ones acting the toughest,
cannot bear to go home alone.

No Authority

Staying out late,
being too loud,
walking too far away while in a crowd
not holding my hand
even when I ask
making mess after mess
not staying on task
never getting to bed at decent times
I don't wake them for breakfast
to avoid their whines
Arguing, fighting,
not doing what they should
I would take away all their privileges
only if I could
how do I punish them for treating me so bad
when I'm the child and they're the mom and dad

No need for a Tour Guide

Off in a dreamland where I play above the clouds,
Where no one scares me or shouts out loud.
A perfect place where everyone gets along,
Laughter in the air as a beautifully composed song.

Safety, care, and concern offered to every child,
The clocks on the wall all point at be free, be wild.
Open arms all around you, willing to share an embrace.
Only smiles you will see upon every face.

Any color you can imagine bouncing with a bright glare.
No signs at every corner, saying look out, stay away, beware.
Knowledge and clarity running like fresh water, pure and clean.
No one to stop you, stand in your way, for what is yours too, to
be seen.

Everyone looking different, as art should be.
Unknown to jealousy or comparison to that which they see.
No amount of currency to determine your wealth,
all among you will share in good health.

A common goal to all that walk in this land,
Never second thoughts of lending a helping hand.

Just like any place you may pay a toll,
By simply discarding all that fouled your soul.

All with breath you once lost will be waiting for you,
no need for a tour guide, you will know what to do.

Breath

Your first one taken is celebrated
It's an occasion
only belonging to you, unable to lend it
careful not to waste it on conflict
Possessing it means you have opportunity
For it to be suddenly taken away, no one has immunity
Treat your time wisely in this life, leave yesterday adorned
Your last one taken shall one day be mourned

Molt

Turning death into birth
Beauty so beautiful without the proper footing,
with your fate you flirt
First Light so bright you could burn
Creatures on fast forward awaiting their turn

Dear Iris,

You look straight into me with your sincere eyes,
Asking nothing in return, sit with me during all my cries.
Without a word spoken, your there to comfort me,
And loudly warn me of all things approaching I cannot see.
Always standing at attention when I feel vulnerable,
I thank you for never leaving my side anytime I am
uncomfortable.
No matter how I look, you greet me with a kiss.
Your love, affection, and feelings, I will never dismiss.
Always eating anything I serve with no complaint,
If it weren't for you pooping on the floor,
I would think you were a saint.

I write

I write when things are tough, a satisfying way to cope,
Reminding others of strength, wanting to promote hope.

I write to make others think,
make some aware they are not alone,
therapeutically admitting,
I too spent time in an unhappy home.

I write to remember or dilute the things I cannot forget.
Trying to let go what could pose an emotional threat.

I write trying to make people laugh, smile, or even shed a tear,
including sentimental thoughts or memories I hold dear.

I write to show who is reading some kind of love,
By relating, passing on a lyrical hug.

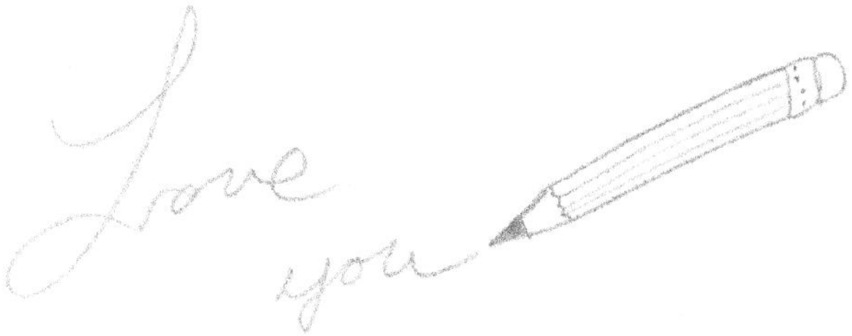
Love
you

My Memphis

where every skin color resides
Where one man with guts, glory, and God on his side
Moved immoral tides.
where I was taught to pray for the sinner, reminded,
I too am one.
where the good stern parents asked after a fight, did you
learn? While stating, nobody won!
where the grandparents already knew before they asked.
where sitting on the front porch will never be part of the past.
where if needed, the teachers moved you to the front
and not the back.
where Love Thy Neighbor will never lack.
where we know, too many young people are dying as
our confidence in humanity depletes.
where we need more Angels and Soldiers in our streets.
where heartache from all the crimes on our hearts,
for others weigh.
where many call home and will continue to love, protect,
and pray.
My Memphis

Grief

Grief is an emotional obstacle course with no time limit.
Days and nights become hurtles to navigate through,
some starting easier than others do.
The main thing to remember is take care of you.
move forward at your own pace not someone else's
guidelines or rules.
No such thing as getting back to your normal
as it no longer exists.
You now live a life while carrying thoughts of
someone missed.

By invitation Only

An Invitation I cannot, will not turn down.
I unapologetically get to wear my frown.
No hats, no streamer,
no invitation to the awesome creative dreamer.
No champagne, no cake,
no invitation to the one strong enough around others to be fake.
I don't know how long I'll be,
the only one who shows is the weak side of me.
Does not matter who I tell,
I'll be alone and the theme is dwell.
I can take my time and still not be tardy,
For no one is waiting, at my Pity Party.

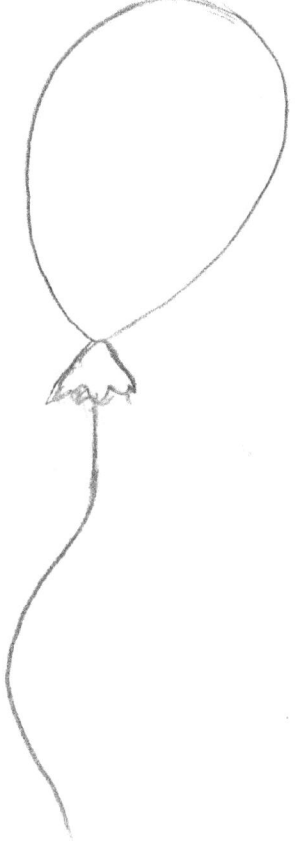

Heirlooms

Just like the waste that exits my body,
I flushed the toxic behavior I've been taught.
I coughed up and spit out the lie of revenge being the right
thing to pursue convinced it grants personal justice
I no longer pick up or hold on to resentment for its
too heavy for me to walk with
I forgive not only others, but also myself.
I will not carry on anything negative I have inherited
determined to rid the next generation of family heirlooms
not labeled by anything other than love

I'll Dance Again

I'll dance again, just like the weekends you didn't show up,
I played pretend.
I brushed my hair like a pretty girl.
I practiced my twirl.
Not too fast
Not to slow
I kept my promise to remember which way
with the song to go.

No matter my age, I will not forget.
I'll always remember, how special our song and dance went.

just like the weekends you didn't show up, I'll play pretend,
until one day Daddy we meet again.

Family Table

Lots of laughter,
Lots of tears,
Many confessions throughout the years.
Sometimes tireless useless fights.
Sometimes serious talks till late in the night.
Crafts for the toddlers,
Rules for the teens,
Lessons for adults on what things really mean.
A place to get help when nowhere else to turn.
A place to get attention if that's something you yearn.
The receiving and giving of helping hands when able.
All of this happens by gathering at the family table.

Emotional Juggler

The anxiousness of a new
The sadness of an old
The one you're trying to avoid
The now you're keeping ahold

The lie you won't admit
The truth that we behold
The conversation you don't want to have
The story that must be told

The actions we decide to take
The noises that were had
The choice to turn a blind eye
The silence that drives you mad

An angel I once called mom

Is she that red bird?
Could she be that butterfly?
Did she send me that rainbow I suddenly see in the sky?
Did she forget about every time I made her sad?
Does she know I asked for forgiveness for making her mad?
Does she remember me?
Will she be the first person I see?
Will she know when I laugh, I'm thinking of our fun?
Does she peek at me during the day from behind the sun?
Whenever I miss her,
I will remain calm,
And remember,
there is an Angel, I once called Mom.

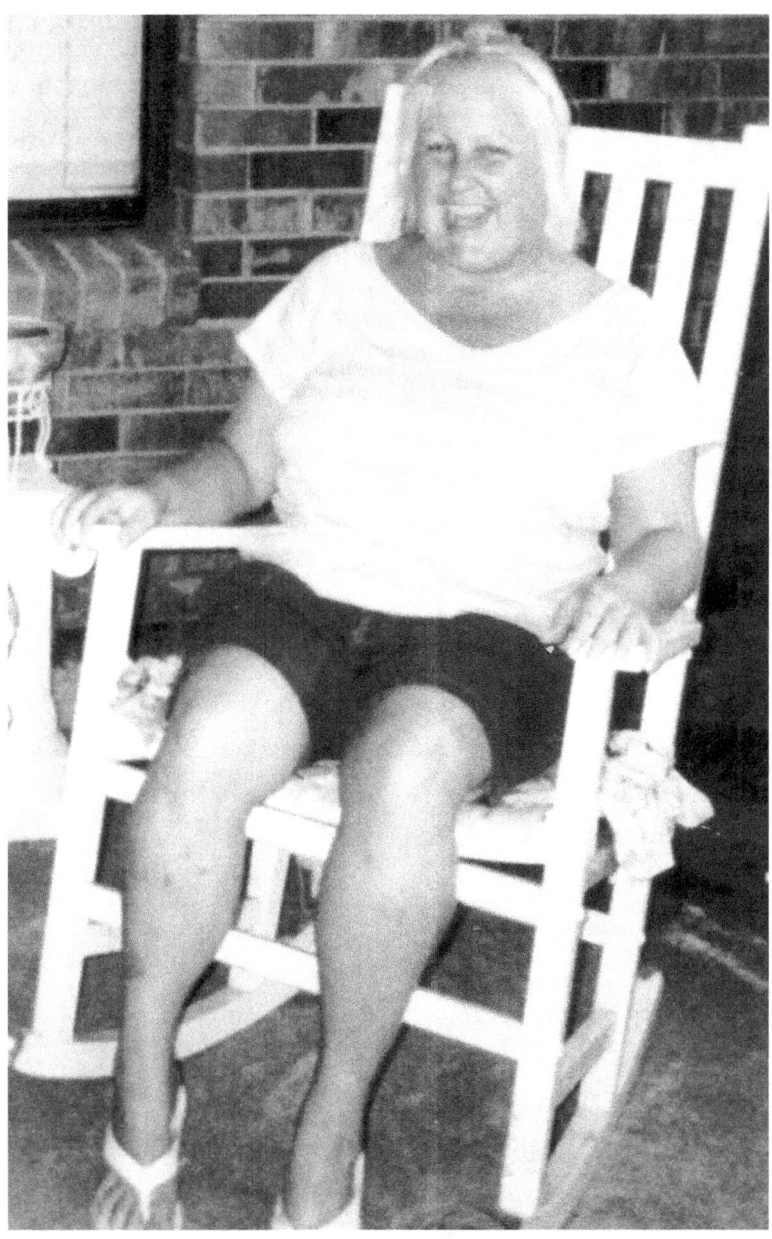

Sentimental affirmation

I get ready to leave my husband and kids for just a bit.
Putting on my best smile with the jeans that barely fit.
Lacing up my shoes I must wear in case of a fight.
Entering the realm of you never know what's going
to happen tonight.
Driving on the way, I wonder, why do I even go?
Will tomorrow be one of the days, he says he didn't know.
Same sad songs making most in the room cry playing
on the juke box.
The establishment, proving bad for business would
be owning any clocks.
Knowing every name with a face, I pretend I'm happy to see.
Looking for that one person, excited for me.
Indicating I'm ready to play the winner, I slam quarters
on the pool table.
Being the only one sober, always ready, and able.
Walking the room among all that talk so much, you must
be a competitor.
Thinking how much longer I can stay in denial; I too have
become a regular.
Oh, there he is, he yelled my name.
I drove all this way, for my 2 seconds of fame.
He gets that glittery gleam in his lonely blue eyes.

So happy to see, I showed up, just for him, always seeming
as it's a surprise.
Wait for it...wait for it....
There he goes, he proudly yells out.
That's my daughter!
smiling so big, he crinkles his nose.
There's the answer
to my wonder. Why I go.

Only yours

I will always be waiting.
I will never walk away.
You can tell me anything.
Count on me night or day.
You can take me anywhere; this you need to know.
I will silently listen to any secret you need to let go.
I will be with you when you say your prayers.
We can grow old together as we wrinkle our outer layers.
You may come and go anytime you please.
I can even comfort you when you fall to your knees.
When needed, I will catch your tears.
I will keep to myself any spoken fears.
I'm not like any lady or fellow.
Just simply your pillow.

When

When you are busy in your world and wearing
your chaotic blinders,
Forsake me not and I shall present you with reminders.

When you are wasting your time on thinking of
what you may lack,
Remember, I am everywhere and will never turn my back.

When you're having a bad day and don't know where to turn,
Pick up my pages, so I can help you look and learn.

When you are fighting your emotions or angry
thoughts in your head,
Give it all to me, so I can lift away your dread.

When you're missing someone gone and bothered
by anxiety or fear,
Don't forget to give me thanks for the time
you held them dear.

When you are loving and caring to another as I am to you,
It's not just in your words, it shall show in all you do.

When you become tired and weary and forget to call out to me,
Do not worry, for tomorrow you have yet to see.

Mortal madness

Now I lay me down to sleep
Time to overthink and begin to weep
Fast forwarding thoughts, deciding which to keep
Financial Visions of drowning in debt
Another mortal fear creating sweat
Flirting with anxiety I'm starting to regret

Overwhelming doubts creeping to the front of my mind
Self-confidence now starts to decline
Needing to slow down, needing to rewind

Heart racing
Up now pacing
Something else to worry about now I'm chasing

Now I lay me down, why can't I sleep......................

Who am I to you?

the coworker you depend on, never giving credit where
credit is due.
the friend you hang out with while single just to
have something to do.

the one you always ask first because I will not say no.
the one you always lie to, thinking I'll never know.

someone you call best friend knowing despite all your flaws I
will not flee.
staying close with enough fakeness, waiting to see me fall, to
suit your jealousy.

the one you talk so negative about and somehow find your way
close as we get seated.
the first person to drop your kid off with, knowing the proper
way he or she will get treated.

The one you repeatedly take from, thinking I don't see.
The relative treated badly, knowing I'll always be there,
because family is important to me.

I hope I'm someone you turned to that helped you get a clue.
And well worth loving for more than what I do.

Bitter sweet space

No wheels moving
Toys in their proper place

Balls stuck on still
No drinks will maybe spill

Swing set empty
Snacks are plenty
Beds stay neatly made

No games to be won
No instruments are loudly played

No one to save from a scary dream
Mud stays outside
Bathroom stays clean

They have all grown up and moved on their way
Now Quiet has taken over my nights and day
I always wondered when this time came, what would
I have to say
With a tear in my eye and joy in my heart, I whisper,
hip, hip, hooray!

Just an aunt

Even though you were not made inside my womb,
In my home, for you, there is room.
Be warned, I will gripe if you do not keep it clean,
this you can assume.

Chores and rules will be plenty and at first you will think you
are doing them for me,
you will display frustration, then slowly, the proudness of your
learning you will see.

I will make sure you know you always have someone,
to count on, be yourself, learn, and have fun.

You and I will not always get it right,
But you can bet, when need be, I will put up a fight.

There will be days you may not like what I have to say,
In time, you will realize all the reasons, with no dismay.

Need to talk, just let me know,
Keep it honest, to help you grow.
Always remember, even though I'm just an aunt,
don't underestimate and think I can't.

Strength

Some think tough is cussing and yelling.
Its keeping to yourself what shouldn't be for your telling.
Some think strong is saying ill kick your ass.
It's never giving a threat, keeping your mouth shut,
showing class.
Some think powerful is starting a physical fight.
It's keeping your hands to yourself, unless you're defending
your life.
Some think scary is making others nervous upon arrival.
It's keeping your posture and appearing as no one's rival.

Stuff

I have cool stuff
Weird stuff
Antiques, midcentury, or new
Collectibles, Knick knacks, I have a slew
Toys, games, glassware from just about anywhere

Corner to corner, an attic full
Boxes, totes, or original packing
Materialistic objects are something I'm never lacking

Some things I searched for and others I happened upon
But none of it should hold importance, I'm not taking it
when I'm gone

Tangled Relations

They arrive,
Chaos consumes the room.
Energy bouncing around,
Like bumper cars aiming for your brain,
all calm energy goes down the drain.
Invited over for dinner, once again, unable to eat.
Telling you the same thing 3 times as if they were on repeat.
Not producing complete sentences as words are in disarray,
Louder and louder,
they continue to speak,
while their own words get in their way.
Taking turns of interrupting,
Looking like neither one of them care,
Louder and louder
Everyone observing can only share in despair.
Not entertained, they suddenly head for the door.
One minute relief they are leaving,
the next,
fear of not seeing the real them anymore.

First

Think before you do,
it could postpone pain for others, including you.
Think before you say,
it could prevent pain that may never go away.
Think before you go,
without a proper goodbye, will the truth they ever know.

God Bless the child

God bless the child that shows up with not much sleep.
God Bless the child in gym that has no strength to compete.
God Bless the child showing up with no food in their belly.
God bless the child by no fault of their own,
got nicknamed smelly.
God bless the child possessing a feature from one parent
hated by the other.
God Bless the child that lives where their creativeness only
gets smothered.
God bless the child that silently works out every problem
on their own.
The bravest thing they do is go back home.
the warmest thing they wear is embarrassment.
The most important things they learn is what not to do.
Their biggest achievement is not treating others like
they get treated too.
God Bless the child that has so little still giving half
to help another in need.
God Bless the child that grew up to work in a profession
where they help other kids safely get freed.

My parents raised

Cain

Suspicion

Voices

Hands

My meals when they would make my stomach churn.

My standards for a relationship

My Expectations for parenting when it's my turn.

A Beautiful person

Full of love for all begins each day,
helping any in their path along the way,
putting others needs first while setting their own astray,
always giving a piece of positive before walking away.
If someone came across your mind while reading the above,
call, check on them, show them some love.

Write - right

It starts with an emotion,
for only there can come the subject to start searching for the
proper words,
to describe what you're feeling.
Without sounding unreal, odd, or dangerous can at times be
absurd.
Molding sentences into a format which is perceived correct by
others,
can make plenty give up from the overwhelming criticism that
kills creativity as negative to art smothers.
So, I will write as I may,
and suggest everyone write when they want, however which
way.
for somehow
some way
it could possibly inspire or uplift,
somebody
some way
someday
A coma here, a period there.
judging another's art, to who is it fair?
to all that share yourself through an expression,
Thank you for showing you care.

Dear Eva,

You got a hug from her on the days I couldn't.
You sat in her room without a spoken word,
never leaving her side your devotion was heard.
She invited you in when no one else was allowed to come near.
She was close to no one, other than you, when she shed a tear.
When it was you that hurt, your love taught her compassion.
When it was you that was sick, your love taught her nurturing.
When it was you that was sad, your love taught her
to quietly console.
I watched you two grow together, adding to each other's soul.
When the time came, you could not go on,
She made the unselfish decision, and made her heart,
your home.

In Loving Memory
of my Grand dog
Eva

Can't be undone

If you are thinking about something that can't be undone
Looking forward to no more sorrow, no more tears
No more sadness, no more fears
Escaping the criticism of all your peers
Please first Think about,
No more moon lights, no more sun
No more laughter, no more fun
Have you ever tried to lend someone your relatable ear
Just once danced or played in the purposeful rain
Created art from your pain
There are lessons in your sorrow, preparing you for tomorrow
so stick around
You may be the only one to help someone else by knowing
what to say
Don't give your chances away to see your better day
You may be the only one to make a difference
along the way

Waste of Strength

To do something cruel
to prove you are not weak
is by far
the weakest waste of strength

Existence

Quiet is the one that screamed for help as a child
and was never heard
Poor is the man with all the money to spare, yet no love
or compassion for another to share
Untrusting is the one betrayed when they gave another
all their care
Happy with their self is the one that feels no need to compare
Sad is the one always making others laugh using their self
to offend
Confident is the one with no need to defend
Lonely is not always the one who lives alone
Accumulating years is not proof you have grown

Imaginal

Could've been
Would've been
Should've been
Nobody will ever truly know
It's merely emotions making ideas grow

Under Construction

When searching for the mortal words to describe the anger
I am feeling
I get lost in the situations of what brought me here
in the first place
starting with the blame upon others, easy, I get lost in how I
think they should have been
after getting exhausted, I realize, I am no better within
time to look at the other one involved
me
I skim across what my part was in making the circumstances
better or worse
Suddenly I have an actual problem-solving plan
I can put into action
Working on the only one I can truly control seems
to be my new attraction

Mother-in-law

Though she's as rude as rude you will ever see
I know she has a heart.
Unfortunately, the words oh well, and I don't care are
how her days start.
She blames everyone for everything that puts a frown
upon her face,
Easily Justifies her son lives here, while she disrespects
my home like it's her own place.
I've never seen someone as negative as she can be,
But when she talks about her daddy, I've never seen someone
sweeter than she.
When she calls, he answers, and within a minute
she tricked him,
before you know it, she's lying and crying, playing the victim.
Since day one, I do not like how she treats and makes me feel,
But... I appreciate, because without her, I wouldn't have him,
let's be real

Unavoidable

Dwindling begins
When wrinkles set in
Your spine develops a bend
Randomly placed hair grows to no end
Each new day gravity makes body parts descend
I hope you did not mistreat others you cannot amend
Someday soon it will get harder to rise from your own rear end
Upon someone else, your errands, and meals will depend

Be still

Never chase,
what needs no permission to move in this life at its own pace.
When you feel love is real,
Give time and space to heal.
For upon return will you know it's true,
safe to share all the rest of you.

In the End

While holding back
To let you be loud,
I heard what I needed to in my silence

While holding back
To let you think your right,
I saw the wrong

While holding back
To let you lie,
I found the truth

While holding back
To let you think your smart,
I became smarter

While holding back
To let you win,
I won

Assure

Yes, it's true,
you should follow your heart,
but
consult your brain,
don't forget that part!

You are Loved

Oppression, depression, guilt, shame,
Walking tall, too proud, or described as lame,
You are Loved.

Deformed, skinny, fat, short,
Body types of many, skin types of any sort,
You are loved.

Fast, slow,
Busy, busy, or nowhere to go,
You are loved.

Doing everything right, or what others think is wrong,
Talented, little, weak, strong,
You are Loved.

Do you know how I know this all to be true?
Because you were imperfectly perfect to be made you.

The Sentence

deters so many

makes you question your own self worth

tells you no more can there be a trusting flirt

heard louder than the inappropriate act performed by another

makes your outgoingness go no further

made it easy to help keep someone's secret

you knew in your face would sure to be thrown

somehow later made the secret your own

scared more than one might agree

can make someone question, was it really because of me?

made the quiet your only true friend

realized the real you, would be the end

turns you from a victim into a defendant

no longer allows you to feel independent

set forth causing more havoc and fury

an attorney is paid to convince the jury

You asked for it

Don't let me slip away

Until we meet again,
I'll be waiting where you left me.
Do not let an expiration be more than a day,
For without my presence, no telling what others might say.
Please know the longer I am without you, I tend to wither,
But I fret not, dirty parts will make you come hither.
I'll stay quiet.
I'll stay calm.
awaiting my existence within in your palm.
Do not neglect or leave me stranded on the
edge of a slippery slope.

Love Always,
Your soap.

Patience Patients

In and out so many come and go
An abundance of emotions from each a steady flow

Anxiety, Anger, Sorrow, Fears
Promises, prayers, hope, tears

Never alone even beside an empty chair
Take a second, give thanks, remind someone you care

All in line for some sort of test
Anxious for answers, needing some rest

Let your faith outweigh any feeling of doom
While sitting still, count your blessings in the waiting room

Stay fun

No matter your age,
make some time,
be goofy as you can be
tell a joke, make up a story
allow your silliness to be set free
Run like a child not knowing where to stop
Get on the ground, try a flip, do a flop
Bubbles, bikes, no destination hikes
While alive
Make it a point, give to yourself all your real likes

Us

You
Me
Him
Her
Them
They

Were
Are
Always will be
One Race
In One Place
Yearning another Day

Worth it

Daddy, when you left, you said you would be back
But you never came

Mr. Knight in shining armor, I dressed and
acted like a princess
But you never came

Dear hero, I was a damsel in distress more than once
But you never came

Hey, first boyfriend, you said you loved me
But never came back

Thank you to all that never showed up, it made me
appreciate him more.
My friend,
my lover,
my husband,
my family,
He never left,
And most importantly, when I tried, he didn't let me.

Angels with an Attitude

Time to get up,
I wake them with a song,
One says hush and the other says I take too long.
My boy is going fast, trying to aggravate my girl,
Her going slower with every outfit taking a twirl.
Changing her mind and wanting to quit,
all because her brother, his food, he spit.
Doing all I can to keep them going,
I act goofy to make them smile,
In my mind, praying they have a good day all the while.
Headed for the door we check backpacks
and grab a water bottle,
Keeping my goal of them moving forward,
staying in full throttle.
Finally in the car and on our way,
we double check spelling words and anything
they might need to say.
Pulling up to school, into the world they must go,
When they turn back to say, Granny I love you! that's
all I need to know.
I will always help them, no matter what their mood,
Life is much better shared among my angels with an attitude.

Anybody

the fanciest purse
no name brand shoes.
most expensive car
no groceries for a meal to choose.

highest paid job or never worked.
biggest wedding or all alone
the best idea or the one that dropped the ball.
traveled the world or unable to leave home.

winning every trophy
possessing a disability
flunking each test
born with excellent mobility.

walking down the red-carpet runway.
Or
sleeping under the busy dirty freeway.
know,
There is no such person as a nobody.
Everyone
is another somebody.

Disorder

Do not mistake depression or anxiety as a meaning of weak.
the thoughts I control are not for the meek.
Be careful to think I may be lazy,
No telling where I'll be next, probably somewhere
most call crazy.
I'm not afraid of others,
its myself, my reactions, why I stay longer under the covers.
Questioning everything that runs through my mind is
exhausting,
Wondering what's wrong with my brain for allowing
entrance of such things.
I know I'm ok if I'm still questioning being deranged.
Certainly, I'm not the only one that.........Well better
not say what I entertain.
Frustrating not being able to explain,
the overwhelming state of mind of constant misunderstood.
Every waking moment, my battle being stuck alone in
my own mental neighborhood.
Emotions to some are easy come and go, switching
channels as if it's just a flow,
To me, they are a stab, twisting in the definitions,
making of another empty hole.

In the House of Abuse

Compliments are scary,
when you know what after actions they may carry.
Asks are really demands,
wrapped with a question mark, which is a dare to deny.
The definition of respect changes every day,
Still, you must look them in the eye.
The home where no matter the level of pain, you may not cry.
Keep breathing,
rest will come in the moments you are left alone.
Quiet and obedient, another day more punishment to
postpone.

Out of the House of Abuse

The end meant I did escape.
The new beginning means with the future I have a date.
For all things I did or did not learn,
I'm proud of my spirit and the gift of discern.

Dear grown up

My fault when you were 2, 5, or 10,
But face it, you're an adult,
you can't blame me for your mistakes again.

Brought up by individuals that love you beyond measure,
No matter what you think of us, being there for you was
our pleasure.

The way you were raised was not perfect or without mistakes,
We always tried, while learning ourselves as we grew with our
own heartaches.

You may hold against us plenty and remember all our boring
rambles,
But let me remind you, time is moving forward, do better, use
us as examples.

I'm sure there is lots you think we did wrong or was not
pleasant,
But one thing is certain my child, I was always trying while
being present.

Anchored by

Anchored by the words scrambling for space in my head
Hoarding all the ones bringing me dread
Convinced no reason venturing towards what is ahead

Anchored by the names called out by others hate
Accepting labels from them all, no debate
Convinced, bury my own, easier to carry their emotional weight

Anchored by abuse once done to me
Questioning daily why this should be
Convinced, my fault, one day I'll see

Anchored by internal fear
Gathered rejection by many deaf external ear
Convinced no outside help reasons would soon be clear

Anchored by doubt to produce what I should
Wondering, waiting for something I could
Convinced someday all this will be understood

After the Heart Attack

The day before, I griped about your snoring.
Tonight, its music to my ears.

The day before, I took for granted our priceless time.
Tonight, I'm praying for many more years.

The day before, I complained about the garage being such a
mess.
Tonight, I decide not to ever bother you again with worthless
stress.

The day before, we argued about who made us late.
Tonight, I assure you, not matter when we arrive, together, it
will be great.

The day before, we fussed about which bill we had to pay.
Tonight, I fall asleep simply looking forward to another day.

The day before, our bad habit was letting our relationship drift.
Tonight, I promise going forward I will treat our love like
a special gift.

The Anxious Wait

Invisible opponents

Your built-up bullet of hate cannot penetrate another
For the pain inside you can never be consumed as so you feel it
The power of your own pain does not go beyond you, know,
your demons are blind to other demons
for you will never know what you're up against until it may be
too late,
so please, teach your inside thoughts to hesitate,
stop the release, defeat it by never giving it permission to
escape.

Farewell

Never letting me leave your sight does not equal you are there
Equal you care
Apologies after the hitting to affection will never compare
If you are capable of love
Let me walk away
All your horrible words, do not say
When you want to physically harm, instead pray
Later, when you are better, and time has passed
Treat yourself and someone good
let me be the last

Toxic Interruption

Lack of respect from the one I choose to love
welcomes destruction
provokes my buried corruption,
returning each yell, each interruption
causes a personal growth deduction,
fights and arguments put on an unhealthy production
the cuss words and name calling feels like a seduction,
flirting with an eruption
the lack of concern causes a relationship obstruction,
disrespectfulness is an abduction to all that makes love secure
without acknowledging, one day the repair could be
too much construction

These hands

With these hands I have whooped some butts
rescued mutts
baby Swaddled
big kids Coddled
Done my part to make things fair
Tried to show every age how much I care
Wiped several tears not only my own
Spent wonderful hours making a house a home
With all that's in me truth be told
as long as i have them, they are here to hold.

Wrong Way

Not far to travel,
I know the short cut way,
each time I go it seems longer I stay.
It's going to cost me and the way-back takes a little longer,
No matter the level, familiar feels comforting, not always
stronger.
Once I get up and leave, I promise myself I will not go back.
only looking forward, a discipline I lack.

The pasture

Flat grassy acres caged by barbwire and electric fence,
Housing honeysuckle bushes galore with every breeze
delivering pleasurable scents.
Overhead air show displaying acrobatic birds
in a safe open space.
Horses running freely, so magnificent, every movement an
example of grace.
An orchestra of winged insects catching speed while teaching
their babies new flaps,
Butterflies, beauty of new beginnings, emerging from their
stunning wraps.
As the sun begins to set, day creatures find their place for the
night to rest,
Out come all the fireflies with their dancing show to impress.
Cicadas and toads exploding all at once with deep
or screeching tones.
You know when the cows and pigs settle in as
echoes carry their moans.
Nocturnal ones taking their turn with the land or in the sky.
For the rest of the night under the moon and stars
glow every awaken eye.

Midnight escapes

The screams wake me,
hers of screeching pleads,
his, the revisiting monster the bottles create.
Heart pounding under the covers, I can only wait and shake,
questioning will she get away this time, an anxiousness I am
afraid I cannot take.
the sudden silence tightens my body with only
my ears still working,
the nervousness causes me uncontrollable painful jerking.
The crashing of objects lets me know he's not done,
we still have a chance, run mommy, run.

Knock Knock

I call from the driveway inquiring who I come home to
my lover, my enemy, my friend?
I like a heads up where the greeting will begin,
anxiously awaiting an answer, more afraid of one day
walking into the end.
These are the times you realize being with one having
borderline personality,
you must also somewhat possess it, to get along accordingly.
I make plans for next week.
When the time comes, to whom will go?
not till then will I find out, I pray its someone I like and know,
more important, I hope it's someone that likes and knows me,
by then, hopefully ill get a clue to which one will agree.
Though it may be tiresome keeping up with the mood swings,
I have to say, It's worth it to have all else love brings.

Unnecessary Living

Children abandoned, youth violence has spread,
Domestic Shooting, mass shooting, kid shooting,
a permanent headline a worldwide dread.

Schools, churches, precincts
Top of the list where fear is making extinct.

Aerosol, glass, bio waste, more plastic,
Assembly line for a new plushie or Knick knack, how fantastic.

The disrespect to our living earth we none have a suitable case.
Wasting our gift of precious opportunities in this emotionally
unstable place.

This land was meant for the living and ready to use
with what is provided,
instead, we let the news, industries, hate, and government
keep us divided.

From trash on the side of the roads to unnecessary
bloodshed in the streets,
We are doing this earth an injustice and causing
our own defeat.

No doubt

Came from the mountain he did,
Been coming and going since he was a kid.
No entrance or exit I ever saw.
Always dressed nice, yet comfy with no flaw.
I sat beside him during our days in school,
that boy answered every question, he ain't no fool.
Once a week he walks about through town,
Not wearing a smile, not wearing a frown.
I sat out front and watched him one day.
Quickly in and out each place with no delay.
first to the bank, came out counting his cash.
next, the cigar shop, up in the air he flicks his ash.
walking by a homeless person begging for change,
he stopped,
reached in his pockets, handed over all he got.
I had to ask him,
why did you give that person so much, you don't know
what they about?
He replied:
I'm quite certain I could be no help to offer up doubt.
Whatever I can spare, I saw it to be proper,
After all,
don't we all have the same father.

Pattern

Each time you hit me; you were hurting yourself more.
You were chipping away at my love, until there could be
no more.
I was there for you, cared for you, knew what you came from.
Stayed longer than I should, pain and fear mixed, made my
hope go numb.
I saw what you did with your abuse.
You regifted it and used it as an excuse.

Proper Introduction

If we all met over the exchanging of thoughts from the heart
onto pages
The world would be more compassionate,
no more misinterpreting each other's faces.
Art tells more, deeper, than the mouth can.
Love through expression is miraculously more beautiful
with no plan.
The internal wonders being shown,
once set free,
some parts of yourself come to be known.

Apology Poem

kids I interacted with when I was young if I was mean or rude.
Teachers, if I ever disrupted your class.
Peers I may have made fun of or put my hands on.
Any place I did not give enough, where respect was due.
Authority I talked back at,
every intentional burned bridge.
all hurt for the sake of revenge
I was far from wise,
for everything to anybody,
I do apologize.

Certainty

My death to you will be louder than all my words throughout
your years.
When missing me and faced with sorrow
Think of my funny or silly ways and create happy tears.

After I'm gone, do not allow for me to go unspoken.
Examples, stories, and lyrics, I left behind as my mortal tokens.

Apologizes for any negative, leave it in the past where it
belongs.
Carry the lighter load of love, do not pass on any wrongs.

My hope has always been, before you,
I Fade away with your hand in mine,
between us,
no goodbye of any kind

Rudeness

Going out in public, it surrounds you everywhere
Sometimes not making a sound, an unfriendly glare
I saw it this morning as soon as I got to work
I heard it at lunch from someone judging another's quirk
Most of the time when I get home, its sitting on the couch
At holidays, I swear, my in-laws must carry extra around
in a pouch
Explaining things to the teenager, it would loudly appear
Ugh………. realizing, it was like looking in a mirror

Acknowledgment

Why does one want a Thank You, what could it possibly do?
I've already completed my act and I didn't do it for me,
I did it for you.

Helping someone is for no reason other than to assist
and make them smile.
How could a simple thank you make it any more worthwhile?

Showing appreciation and recognizing they were there,
Comes from a Thank you,
Making them feel like,
their time,
their efforts,
you care.

Related Acquaintances

Cousin, uncle, aunt, half, step, I don't really know who they are,
no matter their title, they act, from me, they are too far.

Some thinking they are smarter yet could not pass a moral test.
What could earthly righteousness get them at their time of rest?

Thinking one is better because you didn't have my kind of
parent.
Resilience, strength, independence, and humor is worth more
than any amount to inherit.

To the ones that think their time on me cannot be spent,
You taught me, Mine too, wasted, I should try to prevent.

Pushed to the side has taught me a lot, causing
more than one cry,
Thinking I'm not good enough for my relatives,
I no longer live that lie.

I've reached out, called, and wrote, trying my very best,
It's time I move forward, knowing I'm always blessed.

I will carry on with tradition, business as usual,
See you at the next family funeral.

Parent's Love

you wonder why I overreact and let my emotions soar?
my child,
Your anger is my madness
Your happy is my joy
Your pain is my torment
your beauty to me could not be more

Hormonal coaster

Give me a fan, Its too hot!
Oh no, I can't wear this, I'm too old.
No not that haircut, I'm too young.
Turn off the air it's too cold!

That's so cute, I'm going to cry...
Awe that's sweet, I'm going to cry...
Ugh... that makes me mad, I'm going to cry...
Everything causes tears, I don't know why!

I'm bored, I want to do something.
Let's go out! I want to have fun!
You decide, no not there.
I'm canceling my plans, I'm done! I'm done!

I love you so much!
Leave me alone! go away!
It's your fault I feel like this everyday.
Where are you going? what did I say?

In progress

Struggling is part of the self-start up for success in your future.
Gut wrenching pain is part of a process for participation in the
rest of your life.
after sorrow, tears help cleanse and dilute emotions
through your eyes,
making it able to see things more clearly.

Once Upon a Time

someone searching for Love,
found it within.
Now the real journey begins,

Happily, Ever After

This powerful love, made certain to be,

NO END.......

About the Author

Meet Kristina Keith, a Memphis, TN native who has dedicated her life to raising a family and working a 9 to 5 job. Despite putting her passion for writing on hold for some time, Kristina has recently decided at 48 years young, it's time to prove to herself she can do it and wanted to start with her first love, poetry. She takes pride in being there for others and spreading joy through humor. When she's not writing or reading in the bathtub, Kristina enjoys spending time outdoors and introducing her grandchildren to new games, tricks, and jokes.

Kristina's next book "I Met the Boy Named Jack" a Nonfiction, will be coming out in spring 2024.

Any questions, concerns, or suggestions, please contact at:
KristinaKeithWriting@yahoo.com

www.ingramcontent.com/pod-product-compliance
Lightning Source LLC
Chambersburg PA
CBHW070728130626
46553CB00005B/2201